MW00998285

PREPOSITION PRACTICE

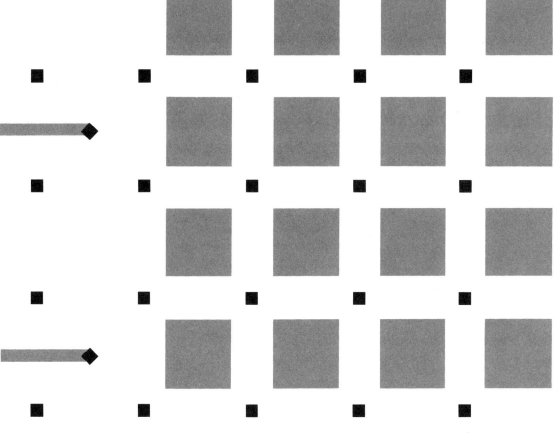

L. L. Keane

Longman

Preposition Practice

Longman, 10 Bank Street, White Plains, N.Y. 10606

Associated companies:
Longman Group Ltd., London
Longman Cheshire Pty., Melbourne
Longman Paul Pty., Auckland
Copp Clark Pitman, Toronto

Distributed in the United Kingdom by Longman Group
Ltd., Longman House, Burnt Mill, Harlow, Essex CM20
2JE, England and by associated companies, branches,
and representatives throughout the world.

Executive editor: Joanne Dresner
Development editor: Debbie Sistino
Production editor: Carol Harwood
Text design adaptation: Acu-Type, Inc.
Cover design: Anne M. Pompeo

Library of Congress Cataloging-in-Publication Data
Keane, L. L. (Leila L.)
    Preposition Practice/L. L. Keane.
        p.   cm.
    ISBN 0-8013-0760-0
    1. English language—Prepositions—Problems, exercises, etc.
    2. English language—Textbooks for foreign speakers.   I. Title.
        PE1335.K43   1991
        428.2'4—dc20   90-47366
                                                                CIP

14 15 CRS 03 02

Contents

Introduction

1 This book groups prepositions into seven sets.
1. Position (Units 1–3)
2. Direction (Units 5–7)
3. Time (Units 9–10)
4. Description (Units 12–13)
5. Adjective + preposition combinations (Units 15–17)
6. Verb + preposition combinations (Units 19–22)
7. Usual phrases (Units 24–26)

2 Each unit is two pages.

3 Each set of presentation units (e.g., Units 1–3) is followed by a Mixed Practice Unit (e.g., Unit 4). These Mixed Practice Units review the prepositions taught in the set, and usually contain some exercises which are more demanding than those in the presentation units.

4 Each presentation unit is self-contained, and therefore these units can be done in any order. It is necessary only to read the information on page 5 before starting.

5 It is possible to use this book for class work, homework, or— since it has an Answer key—for self study.

6 Many units end with a relatively open-ended exercise, in which students can use the language taught to talk or write about themselves, or to exchange information and ideas with a partner.

7 All the work is practiced in meaningful contexts, and much of it deals with the four young people introduced as follows:

Tina is a student. She is twenty years old.

Paul is Tina's brother. He is seventeen years old and is still at school.

Ted is a photographer for Coast to Coast Travel Books.

Sue is an editor in the same company.

Tina, Paul, Ted, and Sue are going to travel around the United States together. They are going to prepare information and pictures for a book called *See the U.S.A.*

①Where? 1

1 The office of Coast to Coast Travel Books is *on* King Street. It is *at* 22 King Street, *in* a large building called the Travel Building. This is *near* Center Park, but rather *far from* Hamilton Park. There is a movie theater *opposite* the Travel Building and a bank *next to* it.

■ Where is the office of (a) Japanese Import Services and (b) the Brazilian Tourist Office?
Use the words below:

on	at	near	far from
opposite		next to	in

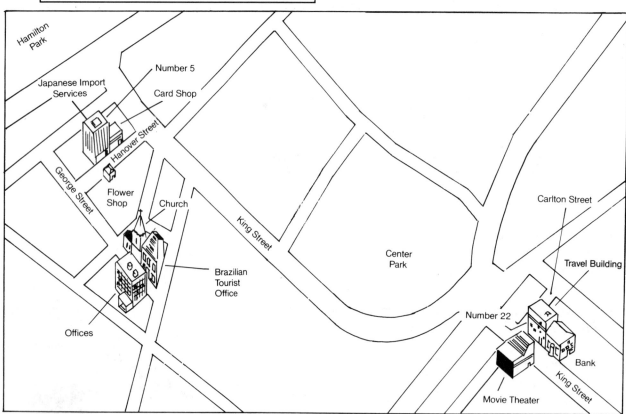

Japanese Import Services is ¹__*near*__ Hamilton Park. The office is ²_____ Hanover Street, ³_____ 5 Hanover Street, to be exact. There is a card shop ⁴_____ it, and a flower shop ⁵_____ it. Japanese Import Services is rather ⁶_____ Center Park. The Brazilian Tourist Office is not ⁷_____ the Japanese Import Services office. It is ⁸_____ 30 George Street. There is a church ⁹_____ it, and some offices ¹⁰_____ it.

2 Sue is talking to Tina on the telephone. "So you and Paul can come on Tuesday! Good! Now, our offices are *in* the Travel Building. We're *on* the third floor. The Regal Restaurant is *above* us. It's *at the top of* the Travel Building, and we're just *below* it. You'll recognize the building easily; there are some flags *on top of* it."

Where is Ted's apartment?
Use the words from column 2 in column 3. Cross out each word in column 2 when you use it.

Column 1	Column 2	Column 3	Column 4
1. Ted's apartment is	on	*in*	Building 3.
2. There are some TV antennas	~~in~~		the building.
3. Ted's apartment is	above		the fourth floor.
4. It is	below		the building.
5. It is	on top of		a coffee shop.
6. Peter's apartment is	at the top of		Ted's apartment.

7

② Where? 2

1 Sue is planning a photo for the book. She has made a drawing and is talking to Ted about it. "Let's have the van *on the left of* the picture, Tina and Paul *in the middle of* the picture, you *on the right,* and all the luggage and equipment *in the front.* And we can have the entrance to the Travel Building *in the back of* the picture."

■ But Ted has a different idea. He says,

"How about having the van ___in the middle of___

the picture, with some trees ² _____ it?

Then we can have Paul ³ _____ , Tina

⁴ _____ the picture, and the luggage

somewhere ⁵ _____ ."

2 Then Sue has another idea. She says,

"Let's have Tina *inside* the van, and Paul *outside* it, standing *beside* it. We can have you *in front of* the van, taking a picture. The luggage can be *around* Paul. And we'll have the Travel Building *behind* you all."

■ Now describe the final picture!

Ted was ¹___inside___ the van, and Tina and Paul

were ² _____ it. The luggage was

³ _____ Tina, who was standing

⁴ _____ the van. Paul was sitting on the

ground ⁵ _____ it, and ⁶ _____ them

all there were some trees.

3 This is Paul's room. He is sitting *in* an armchair, and his guitar is *on* a small chair. He has several pictures *on* the wall, and there are some pictures *on* the ceiling, *above* his bed. He is packing for his trip with Coast to Coast Travel Books, so his bag is *in a corner of* the room. Some of his clothes are *on* the floor. You can see a tree *through* the window.

■ Now complete this description of Tina's room.

Tina has several pictures

¹_____ on _____ the walls of her room,

but she has none ²_____ the

ceiling. There is a light ³_____

her bed. ⁴_____ the window

you can see a roof. Tina's bag is

⁵_____ the floor, there are

some books ⁶_____ a chair,

and her tennis racket is ⁷_____

the room. The family cat is sleeping

⁸_____ the armchair.

4 What about you?

Where is your home? Write about its location, using words from page 6.

_____

_____

_____

_____

5 Now write about a room that you know; for example, your bedroom, a classroom, or the office of a member of your family. Describe its location and some of the things in it. Use words from pages 7 and 9.

_____

_____

_____

_____

③ Where? 3

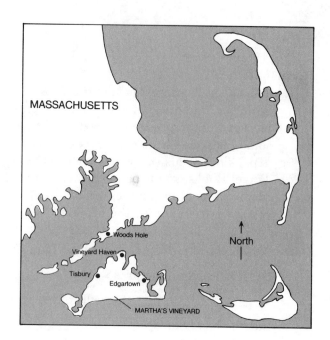

MASSACHUSETTS

Woods Hole
Vineyard Haven
Tisbury
Edgartown
North
MARTHA'S VINEYARD

1 Woods Hole is a town *in* Massachusetts. It is *in the southeast* of Massachusetts, and it is *on* the coast. *Off* the coast, near Woods Hole, there is an island called Martha's Vineyard. This island is *south of* Woods Hole. It is a popular summer resort. Tina and Paul are staying *in* Edgartown, which is *in the east of* the island. Edgartown is about twelve miles *from* Woods Hole.

■ True or false?
Write √ after the true statements, and ✗ after the false statements. Correct the false statements.
1. Woods Hole is in the north of Edgartown.
2. Tisbury is west of Edgartown.
3. Vineyard Haven is in the north of Martha's Vineyard.
4. Woods Hole is off the coast of Massachusetts.
5. Vineyard Haven is south of Tisbury.

_____

_____

_____

2 Complete the description.

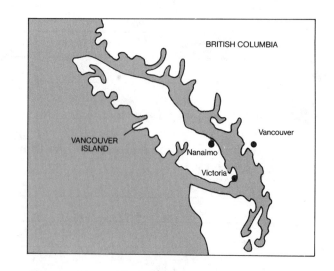

BRITISH COLUMBIA

VANCOUVER
ISLAND
Vancouver
Nanaimo
Victoria

Vancouver Island is an island ¹___off___ the

coast of British Columbia, Canada. It is

²_____ of Vancouver, which is a city

³_____ British Columbia. Victoria is

⁴_____ the coast of Vancouver Island.

Many people live ⁵_____ Victoria.

Nanaimo is ⁶_____ of Victoria. It is

about sixty miles ⁷_____ Victoria.

Nanaimo is ⁸_____ of Vancouver Island.

3 Sue, Paul, and Ted are talking about the kinds of places that they like for their vacations.

SUE: I like climbing, so I like a place *in* the mountains.
PAUL: Well, I like swimming, so I like a place that's *on* the ocean, or *on* a lake or *on* a river. Of course, if the weather's cold, I don't swim *in* the ocean or the lake, but I like being near water.
TED: Well, I like a quiet vacation. I don't like a place that's *on* a busy road.

Write *in* or *on* in column 2.

1. New Orleans is	_____*on*_____	the Mississippi River.
2. There are fish	_____	the Delaware River.
3. Aspen is	_____	the Rocky Mountains.
4. Chicago is	_____	Lake Michigan.
5. New York is	_____	the Atlantic Ocean.
6. People swim	_____	the Gulf of Mexico.
7. Monterey is	_____	the road from San Francisco to Los Angeles.

4 Complete the sentences.

Tina, Paul, Ted, and Sue stayed in motels in many different places. Paul liked motel C because it was ¹ _*on/by*_ a river, and motel D because it was ² _____ a lake. Sue liked motel A because it was ³ _____ a mountain, and she liked motel B even better, because it was right ⁴ _____ a mountain. Ted liked motel F, because it was ⁵ _____ the road, motel E because it was ⁶ _____ a forest, and of course he liked motels A and B too, because they were ⁷ _____ the road.

④ Mixed practice

1 Complete the street map.

Read the description below, and draw the symbols in their correct position.

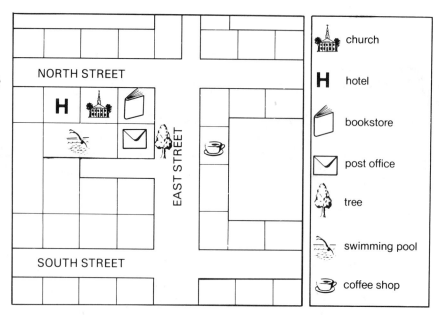

There is a church on North Street. Next to the church, west of it, there is a hotel. Also next to the church, on the corner of East Street, there is a bookstore. Next to the bookstore, just south of it, there is a post office. In front of the post office there is a tree, and behind the post office there is a swimming pool. Opposite the post office there is a coffee shop.

2 How has this store window changed?

Describe the differences.

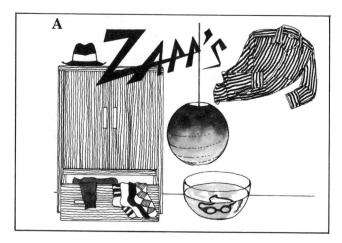

In A the name is ¹_____ of the window, but in B it is ²_____ of it.

In A the dresser is ³_____ of the display, but in B it is ⁴_____ of it.

In A the hat is ⁵_____ the dresser, but in B it is ⁶_____ it.

In A the shirt is ⁷_____ the light, but in B it is ⁸_____ it.

In A the goggles are ⁹_____ the bowl, but in B they are ¹⁰_____ it.

12

3 Write *one* word in each blank.

This is the entrance to Western Recording
Studios. The receptionist is sitting
¹_____ _on_ _____ her chair, with a light
²_____ her. There is a clock
³_____ the wall ⁴_____ her, and a
tall plant in a pot stands ⁵_____ the floor.
A visitor is sitting ⁶_____ an armchair.
The studios are ⁷_____ 53 Alexandra
Street, ⁸_____ the seventh floor.

Grand Bahama Island in the Bahamas is
⁹_____ the coast of Florida. It is about
60 miles ¹⁰_____ the coast, so it is
¹¹_____ the coast. Grand Bahama Island
is 375 miles ¹²_____ Savannah, so it is
quite ¹³_____ _____ Savannah.
Savannah is ¹⁴_____ the coast. It is
¹⁵_____ of Grand Bahama Island, and it
is ¹⁶_____ _____ _____
_____ the United States.

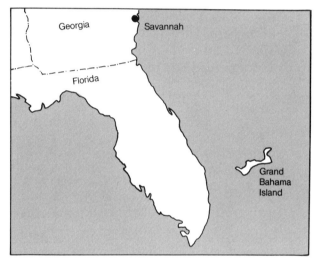

4 Answer these questions, or ask a partner to answer them.
If you could choose . . .

What city, town, or village would you live in? _____

Describe its location. _____

_____

Where would your house or apartment be? _____

_____

How would you arrange your favorite room? _____

_____

_____

Where would you go for your next vacation? _____

Describe the location of this place. _____

_____

5 Direction 1

1 Tina and Paul are in Atlanta in the Visitor's Bureau. An assistant is telling them the way from the Bureau to the Georgia State Capitol. "When you leave this building, turn *left onto* Peachtree Center Avenue. Turn *left* again *onto* Houston Street. Go *along* Houston Street *as far as* Courtland Street and turn *right*. Go *past* Hurt Park, continuing *toward* Georgia Plaza Park. Turn *left onto* Martin Luther King Jr. Drive and turn *right into* the capitol building."

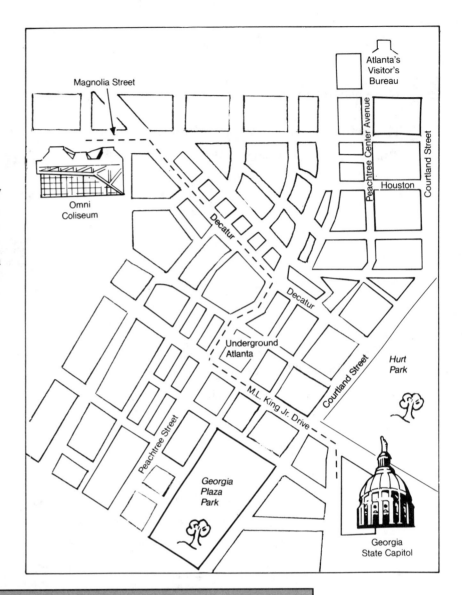

> I turned/ran *onto* Baker Street (= I ENTERED BAKER STREET FROM ANOTHER STREET)
> I turned/ran *into* the building (= I ENTERED THE BUILDING FROM THE STREET)
> I was running *on* Baker Street (= I WAS ALREADY ON BAKER STREET, AND I WAS RUNNING ON IT)

Complete the description of Paul and Tina's walk from the state capitol. It follows the dotted line on the map. Write *one* word in each blank.

Tina and Paul walked [1] __to__ the Omni Coliseum

[2] _____ the capitol building. They crossed Martin Luther King

Jr. Drive and went [3] _____ Martin Luther King Jr. Drive

[4] _____ Peachtree Street. They turned [5] _____ and

walked [6] _____ the underground and continued

[7] _____ _____ _____ Decatur. Then they tur-

ned [8] _____ _____ Decatur and [9] _____ again

onto Magnolia Street. They found the Omni Coliseum on the left.

2 Paul was staying in an old hotel and couldn't find his room.
Complete the sentences.

The elevator stopped *at* the third ¹ f͟l͟o͟o͟r͟ .

Paul got *out of* the ²_____ ,

and went *up* some ³_____ .

Then he went *down* some ⁴_____ .

He walked *along* a ⁵_____ ,

through a ⁶_____ ,

and *into* a ⁷_____ !

The room is He lives	*on* the third floor.	The elevator stopped He got out	*at/on* the third floor.

3 Tina couldn't find her room either. She walked:

¹ o͟u͟t͟ o͟f͟ the dining room,

²_____ some stairs,

³_____ a hallway,

⁴_____ the lobby,

⁵_____ the lobby,

⁶_____ some stairs,

⁷_____ an arch,

and then ⁸_____ the dining room again!

6 Direction 2

1 *across* ⊞→ something flat (e.g., a road or railroad tracks)

over ⌒→ if the path or road goes up and then down (e.g., because of a hill or a bridge)

through 〰→ something that rises on both sides (e.g., tall grass, woods, a town)

■ The dotted line (. . . . .) shows a path in the country. Describe where it goes.

The path goes ¹ <u>past</u> a church, ² _____ the woods, ³ _____ part of a river, ⁴ _____ a bridge, ⁵ _____ a hill, ⁶ _____ some railroad tracks, and ⁷ _____ a road.

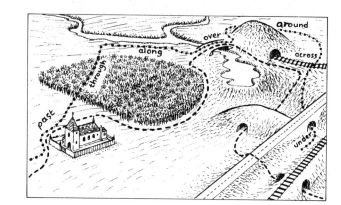

2 But Tina and Paul went a different way. The broken line (— — — —) shows where they went. Describe their walk.

They went ¹ <u>past</u> the church, ² _____ the woods, ³ _____ the bridge, ⁴ _____ a stream, ⁵ _____ a tunnel, ⁶ _____ a road, and ⁷ _____ the railroad tracks.

3

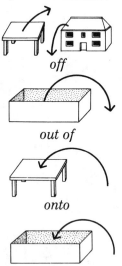

off

off
(a) from a flat surface, e.g., a table or a hard chair
(b) down from, e.g., a roof

out of

out of
from inside something, e.g., a box or an armchair

onto

onto
from a place to a surface, e.g., a table or a hard chair

into

into
from one place to the inside of another, e.g., a room or some water

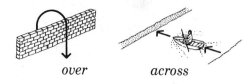

over *across*

over/across
from one side to the other; usually *over* if you go up and then down, e.g., to climb *over* a wall

Paul was at an adventure camp. Fill in the blanks to say where he went.

Paul fell ¹___*off*___ a bridge ²_____ a river. He swam

³_____ the river, then climbed ⁴_____ it, and

climbed ⁵_____ some rocks. He ran ⁶_____ a field

and jumped ⁷_____ a gate. There were some cows in that

field, so he climbed ⁸_____ a pile of stones, and then

jumped ⁹_____ the stones, ¹⁰_____ the ground on

the other side of the fence.

7 Direction 3

1

She flew/went/ traveled, etc. She came She got	to	Chicago, Hawaii, Japan
She left	for	
She arrived	in	
She arrived (NEVER: She arrived to)	at	Bronxville (e.g., AT THE TRAIN STATION, AT THE AIRPORT, AT THE RESTAURANT, ETC.)

These are some of Marco Polo's travels from Venice.
Write *at, in, to,* or *for* in column 2.

1. In 1271 Marco Polo left   __for__   Persia.

2. Some time later he arrived   _____   China.

3. In 1272 he got   _____   Tibet.

4. In 1292 he went   _____   India.

5. In about 1294 he went back   _____   Persia.

6. He arrived   _____   Tabriz in 1294 or 1295.

7. At the end of 1295 he came back   _____   Venice.

2 A young tennis player is telling Tina about her travels.
Write *in, at, to,* or *for.*

"Last year I went [1]___to___ about twenty different countries. I

went [2]_____ Japan for the first time. I came [3]_____ the

United States for the first time in 1985. We had a rather difficult trip

this time. Our plane arrived [4]_____ San Francisco at 2:00 p.m.,

but our luggage got [5]_____ San Francisco three hours later.

The car from the airport broke down, so we arrived [6]_____ the

city itself several hours late. The next day we left [7]_____ New

York, and arrived [8]_____ Kennedy Airport without any

problems, luckily."

3 Look at the map and read about Tina and Paul's bicycle ride.

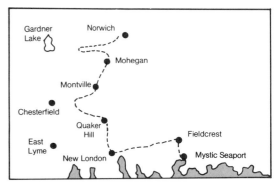

One day, Tina and Paul bicycled from Mystic Seaport to Norwich, Connecticut. First they rode north *as far as* Field Crest. Then they traveled west *toward* East Lyme, going *through* New London. It was about 10:00 a.m. when they rode *into* Quaker Hill, so they had a cup of coffee there. They were riding *out of* Quaker Hill when Tina got a flat tire.

| They bicycled *out of/into* Mystic Seaport (IF WE THINK OF THIS PLACE AS AN AREA) |
| They bicycled *from/to* Norwich, Connecticut (IF WE THINK OF THIS PLACE AS A POINT ON A TRIP) |

Complete the description of Tina and Paul's bicycle ride, using prepositions from the passage and table above.

After Tina and Paul had fixed the tire, they rode northwest
1 *toward* Chesterfield. Then they went north and rode

2 _____ Montville. They continued

3 _____ the town and were

riding 4_____ Mohegan when Paul got a flat tire. So it

was 11:30 when they finally rode 5_____ Mohegan;

then they made a wrong turn and began riding 6_____

Gardner Lake. Altogether the ride 7_____ Mystic

Seaport 8_____ Norwich took them almost four

hours.

4 Describe an interesting trip—real or imaginary—in your country or abroad. Use these verbs (in any order), with a suitable preposition after each one:

| traveled   left   arrived   came   got   went |

_____

_____

_____

_____

_____

_____

⑧ Mixed practice

1 Tina and Paul took a walk in a small town in upstate New York. Complete this description of their route, using the prepositions below.

along	through	past
toward	as far as	onto
across	around	over

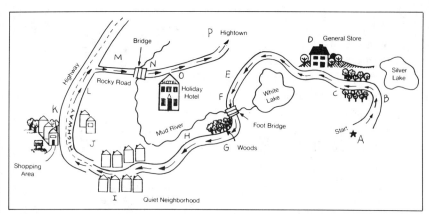

A–B The route goes ¹___toward___ Silver Lake, then turns and goes back

C ²_____ some woods, going

D ³_____ a general store.

E It goes ⁴_____ White Lake,

F ⁵_____ a small foot bridge, ⁶_____ the Mud River,

G ⁷_____ some more woods,

H–I then ⁸_____ the Mud River, going ⁹_____ a quiet neighborhood.

J It turns ¹⁰_____ a main road, and

K goes ¹¹_____ a shopping center.

L–M It goes ¹²_____ the highway, ¹³_____ the Mud River.

M–N Then it turns ¹⁴_____ a small country road, going ¹⁵_____ the river again.

N–O It goes ¹⁶_____ a bridge, and ¹⁷_____ a hotel,

P ¹⁸_____ Hightown.

2 Describe the burglar's actions, using the prepositions below:

into	into	in	onto	on	out of	from	off	up	down	over	across	through

He climbed ¹__up__ a drainpipe,   ²_____ a railing,   and ³_____ a balcony.

Then he got ⁴_____ a bedroom, ⁵_____ an open window.

There he found a necklace ⁶_____ a drawer.

He took some rings ⁷_____ a box,

and two candlesticks ⁸_____ a small table.

(All this time he had been walking ⁹_____ a carpet that was connected to a burglar alarm.)

Then he slid ¹⁰_____ the drainpipe,

ran ¹¹_____ the house

¹²_____ the lawn,

¹³_____ a hill, and

¹⁴_____ the arms of a police officer.

3 In column 3, write the correct preposition from column 2.

1. They came	for	___to___	Honolulu last week.
2. They arrived	in	_____	Hawaii a month ago.
3. Next, they're going	to	_____	Japan.
4. They're leaving		_____	Japan on Tuesday.
5. They're going		_____	Tokyo.
6. They'll arrive		_____	Tokyo on Wednesday.
7. They'll come back		_____	Hawaii next month.

21

9 When? 1

1	*in*	1989 (= A YEAR) (the) winter (= A SEASON) April (= A MONTH)	*on*	Friday (= A DAY OF THE WEEK) New Year's Day/my birthday (= A PARTICULAR DAY) April 8 (= A DATE)
	Note We say *in* April, but *on* April 8.			
	at	Easter/Christmas (= THE PERIOD, NOT THE DAY ONLY)		

Complete this summary of events in San Antonio.

¹ _In_ 1989, there were many public events in San Antonio ² _____ the winter and spring. For example, ³ _____ January there was a concert (it was ⁴ _____ Saturday, January 28), and ⁵ _____ March there were three big events. ⁶ _____ the summer and fall there were fewer events. ⁷ _____ July fourth there were fireworks, and ⁸ _____ a Sunday ⁹ _____ September there was a jazz festival. ¹⁰ _____ October 29 there was an Octoberfest. Of course, there were many celebrations ¹¹ _____ Christmas and ¹² _____ New Year's Eve. There were many similar events ¹³ _____ 1990.

Calendar of Events 1989

SAN ANTONIO

Country Music Concert
Sat., January 28

Tennis Tournament
Feb. 27–March 4

Street Parade
Sat., March 11

Spring Fair
March 18–19

Carnival
May 19–21

Fireworks
Tues., July 4

Jazz Festival
Sun., September 24

Octoberfest
Sun., October 29

2

> There are no prepositions before *last, next, this,* or *every:*
> There were many events in San Antonio *last year*.
> There's a carnival *next Sunday*. It's taking place *this month*. It happens *every year*.

Paul is writing to a friend. In each blank, write a preposition or put a dash (—).

I'm sorry we weren't here ¹___*in*___ March! There aren't so many events ²___—___ this month, but there's a carnival ³_____ next Sunday. ⁴_____ Friday we're going riding. (Do you remember? I took horseback riding lessons ⁵_____ last summer.) I'd like to be here ⁶_____ September, when there's a big jazz festival. They have the festival ⁷_____ every September.

3

in the morning/evening (= A PART OF A DAY)	*at* 6:00/noon/night (= A TIME)

Here is the next part of Paul's letter. In each blank, write *in, at,* or put a dash (—).

Yesterday we went to a health club ¹___*in*___ the morning. We started playing racquetball ²_____ 10 o'clock, had lunch ³_____ 12 o'clock, and ⁴_____ the afternoon we played basketball and then swam. ⁵_____ the evening we went to a disco, and I got to bed ⁶_____ 2 o'clock in the morning.

After breakfast ⁷_____ this morning we rented bikes and rode around San Antonio. We're having a rest now, but ⁸_____ this evening we're going to a concert, which begins ⁹_____ 8:30.

23

10 When? 2

1 Tina's life

1970	Born in Baltimore.
1972	Brother Paul born.
1974	Family moved to New York.
1975	Tina started school.
1984	Began high school.
1986	Started guitar lessons.
1988	Graduated high school. Then worked in a bookstore.
1988	Began college.
1990	Still at college. Still plays the guitar.

Examples
Tina lived in Balitmore *from* 1970 *to/until* 1974.
She was born *before* Paul.
She started school *after* her fifth birthday.
In 1989, she had been playing the guitar *for* three years.
She had been playing it *since* 1986.
She began playing it *during* high school.

Notes
We use *for* with time periods which we measure or count:
 for five years/four weeks/three days/two minutes
We use *during* with time periods which we do **not** measure or count:
 during lunch/high school/1986
We use *since* with a point in time:
 since 1986/last March/six o'clock

Complete these statements about Tina's life. Imagine that it is now 1990.

1. Tina lived in Baltimore ____for____ four years.

2. She has lived in New York _____ sixteen years.

3. She has lived there _____ 1974.

4. She started school _____ the family's move to New York.

5. She attended high school _____ 1984

   _____ 1988.

6. She worked in a bookstore _____ her summer vacation.

7. She worked there _____ two months.

8. She has been at college _____ two years.

9. She has been playing the guitar _____ four years.

10. She has been playing it _____ 1986.

2

> Tina was at school *from* 1975 *to/until* 1988.
> She was at school *until* (NOT *to*) June 1988.
> She had left school *by* July 1988. (*by* = BEFORE, NOT LATER THAN)

Use each preposition from column 2 in column 3.
Cross out each word in column 2 when you use it.

1. Tina lived in Baltimore	to	_until_	1974.
2. She had started school	to	_____	her sixth birthday.
3. She worked in a bookstore from July 1988	by	_____	September 1988.
4. She'll stay at college	by	_____	June 1992.
5. She'll leave college	by	_____	the summer of 1992.
6. She says she's going to work hard	~~until~~	_____	graduation!
7. She'll forget this promise	until	_____	next weekend.
8. Last night she danced from ten p.m.	until	_____	two in the morning.

3 Answer these questions, or ask your partner to answer them. Use the prepositions in italics in your answers.

1. *For* how long have you lived in your present home?

   I have lived in my present home ____for_____

2. So that is *since* when?

   That's since _____

3. *Since* when have you been learning English?

   _____

4. *Until* what date are you going to attend English classes?

   _____

5. *By* what date will you stop studying altogether?

   _____

11 Mixed practice

1 At a travel agent's.
Write a suitable preposition in each blank.

"Right! your plane leaves [1] *at* 2:00. You should check in 1½ hours [2]_____ departure time, so you need to be at the airport [3]_____ 12:30. You can wait in the departure lounge [4]_____ check-in time [5]_____ departure time.

  You'll probably wait there [6]_____ about 1:50. Now, about getting to the airport. There's an airport bus that leaves the terminal [7]_____ 11:00. You could catch that. I know there's always a lot of traffic going to the airport [8]_____ the morning, [9]_____ about 8:00 [10]_____ about 10:00. However, you'll be going [11]_____ that period, so you'll be OK."

2 In a coffee shop.
Write a dash (—) or one of the prepositions below in each space:

from	for	during	since	to	until

"Where have you been? We agreed to meet at 2:30. I've been waiting for you [1] *for* hours! Well, not exactly hours, but [2]_____ 2:35. Let me see— [3]_____ 2:35 [4]_____ now: that's forty minutes. I've drunk three cups of coffee [5]_____ that time and got very bored. If I'd brought a book I could at least have been reading [6]_____ forty minutes. Anyway, what's your excuse?"

  "My excuse? I've been waiting for you [7]_____ thirty minutes in the street. We agreed to meet on the street corner, didn't we? Anyway, [8]_____ next week let's meet [9]_____ Tuesday. That's easier for me than Wednesday. See you [10]_____ next Tuesday, then."

"What? Are you going already? Aren't you going to stay

^{11}_____ a few minutes?"

"No, I can't! I have a dentist's appointment ^{12}_____ this

afternoon. I'll have to wait ^{13}_____ Tuesday for your news!"

3 A reporter has been interviewing a pop star and has made these notes. Use the notes to write his article. The date of the article is April 10, 1990.

<u>Contessa</u>
5·10·65 Born in Pasadena, California
1970-82 School (hated it).
1975 Began singing, in church choir (left 1980).
1980 Had already made 3 records! (for church).
1982 Began singing with local group.
  (The Pebbles). (Left group 1984).
84·83 Sang in show in Las Vegas. Mammoth
  Records producer in audience.
Two weeks later: signed contract with Mammoth
Records. Still under contract with Mammoth.
1988 & 1989: Gold records.
Says:" Have been singing for other people for 15
years, but really sing for myself."
Plans to make third gold record ("not later than
25th birthday!") Checked charts last Saturday
- seems possible.

_____

_____

_____

_____

_____

_____

_____

_____

_____

_____

12 How?

1 Ways of traveling

In general		When talking about particular vehicles
by	bike/motorcycle/car/ van/truck/train/plane/ air/bus/ship	*on* his/that, etc. bike/motorcycle *in* my/this, etc. car/van/truck *on*[1] the train/plane/bus/ship
	boat	*on* the boat (if a large boat) *in* the boat (if a small boat)
on	foot[2]	
Examples I like traveling *by* bike. I traveled around Italy *on my cousin's* bike.		
Notes [1]It is possible, but less usual, to say *in* the train, etc. [2]It is more common to use the verb *walk*: I went to school *on foot*. I *walked* to school.		

■ Ted is talking about a vacation which he had once in the United States.
Write prepositions from the table above in these blanks, adding other words if necessary (e.g., *the*, *a*).

In New York I went around ¹_____on_____ foot mainly. You can visit the Statue of Liberty ²_____ boat, and ³__on the__ boat I met another photographer. We decided to go together to San Francisco ⁴_____ bus, because it's cheaper than going ⁵_____ train or ⁶_____ plane. Altogether we spent four days and nights ⁷_____ bus. We wanted to go around San Francisco ⁸_____ car; a cousin of mine lent me his car, but after we'd been ⁹_____ car for only a few hours, it broke down. By this time it was midnight, and we started to go back to my cousin's house ¹⁰_____ foot, but a truck driver stopped and took us back ¹¹_____ truck. I came back to New York ¹²_____ air, and I can tell you I was too tired to talk to anyone ¹³_____ plane! I think it would be great to do the trip from New York to San Francisco ¹⁴_____ motorcycle. There's a book about a man who took his small son right across the United States ¹⁵_____ old motorcycle.

2 How things are made

Things can be made . . .

of MATERIALS OR SUBSTANCES: This table is made *of* wood.
out of A COMPLETELY DIFFERENT THING (one object is changed into another): She is making a dress for her daughter *out of* some old curtains.
by PEOPLE: The Pyramids were built *by* people who lived a long time ago.
with (= using) TOOLS AND OTHER AIDS: On the beach we built sandcastles *with* our pails and shovels.

In San Antonio, our four friends made their own costumes for a costume party.
Read the first description. Then complete the other descriptions, using the correct prepositions.

safety pins

glue

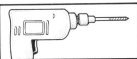
drill

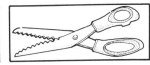
scissors

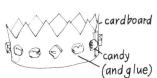
Paul's crown

This crown is made *of* cardboard. The jewels on it are made *out of* candy. It was made *by* Paul. Paul stuck on the candy *with* glue.

Tina's dress

This dress is made ¹ _out of_ a trash bag, which is made ² _____ black plastic. The dress was made ³ _____ Tina. She cut out the armholes and neckline ⁴ _____ some special scissors.

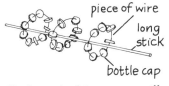
Ted's "musical instrument"

This "musical instrument" was made ⁵ _____ Ted. It is made ⁶ _____ a long stick, some pieces of wire, and some bottle caps. The bottle caps are made ⁷ _____ metal, so they make a noise. Ted made the holes in them ⁸ _____ a drill.

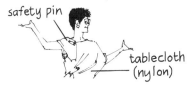
Sue's dress

This dress is made ⁹ _____ two tablecloths. They are made ¹⁰ _____ nylon, so it's rather hot. It was made ¹¹ _____ Sue. She put it together ¹² _____ safety pins.

13 What are they like?

1 He/She is a person . . .

of[1] (AGE)	with (PHYSICAL CHARACTERISTICS)
about 20	a big smile
about 16	an amazing hairstyle
at least 25	curly hair
about 18	a small moustache

[1]**Note**
Do not use "years" or "years old" after *of*.

in (THINGS WE WEAR)	with (THINGS WE CARRY)
a small black hat	a funny football
dark glasses	a strange bag
a white blouse	a cane
a football shirt	a guitar

At the costume party.
Read the first description. Then describe the other people, using
phrases from the table.

A man *of* about 20, *with* a big smile, *in* a football shirt, and *with* a
funny football.

A girl of [1]*about 18* , with [2]_____ , in [3]_____ ,
and with [4]_____ .

A man of [5]_____ , with [6]_____ , in [7]_____ ,
and with [8]_____ .

A girl of [9]_____ , in [10]_____ , with [11]_____
and with [12]_____ .

2	*as* (FOR A PERSON'S JOB OR ROLE)	*like* (TO COMPARE THINGS)
	She works *as a reporter*. He joined the team *as an extra player*.	She ran *like the wind*. He looks *like his father*.

Note
You must use *a/an* before the name of a job:
    She works *as a reporter* (not "as reporter")

Things that people said at the party.
Write *as* or *like*.

1. TINA: "Goodness! You look [1] <u>like</u> Charlie Chaplin. And you dance [2]_____ him too!"

2. TED: "I once worked in a movie theater [3]_____ an usher. I managed to look [4]_____ an actor, but of course I didn't get paid [5]_____ one."

3. SUE: "I can't dance all night [6]_____ you! I'm not here [7]_____ a tourist, you know! I'm working. Anyway, I'll sleep [8]_____ a baby tonight."

4. PAUL: "Ted's with us [9]_____ our photographer. I'd like to take photos [10]_____ his! His camera's [11]_____ a computer!"

3 Using *of*, *with*, and *in*.

1. Describe yourself: your age, a physical characteristic, something you are wearing, and something you are holding or using.

I am a man/woman/boy/girl _____

_____

_____

_____

_____

2. Describe someone in your class in the same way. Ask your neighbor to guess whom you have described.

_____

_____

_____

_____

_____

[14] Mixed practice

1 Three presents.
Write *as, like, of, out of,* or *by* in the blanks.

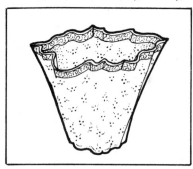

1. This looks ¹___like___ a handkerchief. It is made ²_____ china, and you can use it ³_____ a vase. It was made ⁴_____ an artist.

2. This was made ⁵_____ a golf ball and some pieces of paper. You can use it ⁶_____ a paperweight, and it looks ⁷_____ a duck.

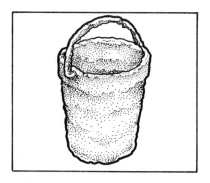

3. This was made ⁸_____ a child, ⁹_____ a plastic container, some wire, and moss. You can use it ¹⁰_____ a planter.

2 Bus? Car? Train? Boat? Air? Or . . . ?
Say how one can travel from your capital or your home to three other places.

1. You can travel from _____ to _____ by _____ , or by _____ or by _____ .

2. _____

_____

3. _____

_____

3 Someone broke the window of a house and stole some silver. Three people say they saw the robbery, but they have told very different stories to the police. Complete each description with prepositions.

WITNESS A: "He was a man ^{1}___of___ about 20, ^{2}_____ long dark hair, ^{3}_____ jeans. He was wearing a mask made ^{4}_____ a stocking, and he looked ^{5}_____ a gangster. He broke the window ^{6}_____ a brick, and escaped ^{7}_____ a bicycle. It looked ^{8}_____ a racing bike."

WITNESS B: "She was a woman ^{9}_____ about 30, ^{10}_____ short, dark hair, ^{11}_____ a sweatsuit. She was wearing a sort of mask made ^{12}_____ cardboard. She broke the window ^{13}_____ a bottle, and escaped ^{14}_____ a motorcycle. She drove that motorcycle ^{15}_____ a madwoman!"

WITNESS C: "He was a man ^{16}_____ about 40, ^{17}_____ very little hair, ^{18}_____ a dark suit. He looked ^{19}_____ a businessman, and he used his newspaper ^{20}_____ a sort of mask. He escaped ^{21}_____ a large, black car."

4 Say how you and three other people (family, friends, or other students) traveled to work today.

1. I came to college/school today _____
2. _____
3. _____
4. _____

15 Adjectives + prepositions 1

1

He was good/kind, etc. *to* my brother (= A PERSON)

He was good/kind, etc. *about* my brother/
his hat/what my brother did (= AN EVENT
OR A SITUATION)

It was good/kind, etc. *of him to* excuse
my brother.

A TV commercial. A cowgirl is speaking to a cowboy.
Write *to, about,* or *of* in each blank.

"Ed, darling, what's happened to you? You used
to be rude [1] _____to_____ my parents, but now
you're so polite [2]_____ them. You used to
be nasty [3]_____ my cooking, but now
you're nice [4]_____ it. You used to be
unkind [5]_____ my small brother, but now
you're very kind [6]_____ him. You were
very kind [7]_____ your hat; it really was
nice [8]_____ you to keep calm
[9]_____ that! You used to be mean
[10]_____ the farm workers, but now you're
generous [11]_____ them. In fact, you used
to be unpleasant [12]_____ everybody and
[13]_____ everything, but now you're
pleasant [14]_____ everybody and
[15]_____ everything. Tell me, Ed, what's
happened?"

"What's happened, honey? I've discovered
Shavex Shaving Cream! It sure was good
[16]_____ you to give me that superb cream
for my birthday!"

2

pleased impatient careless patient careful[1] angry	*with* her daughter/the present (= PEOPLE OR THINGS) *about* the match/the heavy traffic (= EVENTS OR SITUATIONS)
right sorry[2] wrong worried	*about* him/the present/the match/the traffic (= PEOPLE, THINGS, EVENTS, OR SITUATIONS)

Notes
[1]You can also say *careful of:* Be careful *of* the traffic (= BE CAREFUL THAT IT DOES NOT HARM YOU)
[2]I'm sorry *about* your father (= I AM SORRY THAT HE HAS DIED)
 I'm sorry *for* your father (= I PITY HIM [BECAUSE YOU HAVE TREATED HIM BADLY, ETC.])

Paul and Tina are at a tennis camp in Pennsylvania.

Paul is writing to his cousin. Fill each blank with *one* word.

1. My tennis racket's really good. I'm very pleased __with__ __it__ .

2. But I've lost three tennis balls. I'm so angry _____ _____ .

3. Now I have only three. I'll be careful _____ _____ .

4. Our first coach used to shout at us. He was very impatient _____ _____ .

5. Then he left. We weren't sorry _____ _____ .

6. The new coach is excellent. He's very patient _____ _____ .

7. At first I thought he was no good, but I was wrong _____ _____ .

8. I won a match today. I'm very pleased _____ _____ .

9. My big match is tomorrow. I'm not worried _____ _____ .

10. You said that Pennsylvania is nice. You were right _____ _____ .

3	to be pleased/worried, etc. *about*	*doing* something *not doing* something

Example
I'm pleased *about being* here, but I'm sorry *about not seeing* you.

Paul is writing to his parents now.
Write *one* word in each blank. Use the verbs in italics.

I *lost* three tennis balls yesterday. I was sorry [1] __about__ __losing__ __them__ . I didn't *find* any of them; I was angry [2] __about__ __not__ __finding__ __them__ . We have to *wait* for our classes. We have to be very patient [3]_____ _____ _____ _____ . I *won* a match today. I was pleased [4]_____ _____ _____ . I'm *playing* in a bigger match tomorrow. I'm not worried [5]_____ _____ _____ _____ . I haven't *written* to you very often. I'm sorry [6]_____ _____ _____ _____ _____ more often.

16 Adjectives + prepositions 2

1

bad good quick slow clever efficient	*at*	afraid fond proud sure tired	*of*	interested qualified	*in*

Examples
She's good *at* arithmetic but slow *at* algebra.
I'm afraid *of* dogs, but I'm fond *of* cats.
He's interested *in* computers and qualified *in* mathematics.

Tina's letter from Pennsylvania.
Write *at, of,* or *in.*

Dear Lucy,

Paul and I can canoe now! At last! So we're very proud
[1] __of__ ourselves. Canoeing is a great sport, especially in a
river full of rocks! Of course, we're not very good [2]_____ it
yet, and at first we were really bad [3]_____ it. We fell into
the river at least ten times, I'm sure [4]_____ that. I'm not
afraid [5]_____ the river, but I'm not fond [6]_____
very cold water! Getting into the canoe was rather difficult too,
but we're pretty quick [7]_____ that now. So we're enjoying
ourselves, but we're very tired [8]_____ the rain here. It's
been raining for three days.

Please write. I'll be interested [9]_____ your news.

All the best,

Tina.

2 | to be bad *at*/afraid *of*/interested *in*, etc. *doing* something

Examples
He's good *at swimming* and *running*.
She's fond *of driving* fast cars.
He's interested *in helping* other people.

When Sue first met Tina and Paul in New York, she asked them some questions. Look at her notes and complete her questions.

1. Are you fond ___of getting up early ?___
   _____

2. Are you good _____
   _____

3. Are you afraid _____
   _____

4. Are you interested _____
   _____

5. Are you clever _____
   _____

1. Get up early.
2. Put up a tent.
3 Try dangerous sports.
4. Meet lots of different people.
5. Learn new skills.

3 What about you, your family, and friends? Or what about your partner? Write sentences like this:
(very interested)   I'm *very interested in* guitar music.
(.........) is *very interested in taking* photographs of wild animals.

(very interested) _____

(qualified) _____

(clever) _____

(very slow) _____

(good) _____

(very bad) _____

(afraid) _____

17 Adjectives + prepositions 3

1

bad good	*for* + noun		capable fond	*of*	+ noun + *doing something*
famous responsible grateful sorry	*for*	+ noun + *doing something*	proud sure tired		
			bored	*with*	

Examples
I'm sorry *for* breaking the dish (= I APOLOGIZE).
I'm sorry *for* the animals in the cage (= I PITY THEM).
Fruit is good *for* your health.
She's famous *for* her parties/*for giving* good parties.
He's capable *of* good work/*of doing* good work.
I was bored *with* the talk/*with listening* to the talk.

■ Find the right ending for each sentence.
Write your answers below.

A. Children are usually fond
B. Rome is famous
C. Children usually get bored
D. They also usually get tired
E. Too much coffee is bad
F. We feel sorry
G. Parents are usually proud

1. for its beautiful buildings.
2. of adults' conversations.
3. for the nerves.
4. of their children.
5. for sad people.
6. with reading long books.
7. of eating ice cream.

A. __7__ , B. _____ , C. _____ , D. _____ , E. _____ , F. _____ , G. _____

2 Paul and Tina are at a music summer school. Paul is talking to
Vicky, one of the teachers.
Complete the changed versions of their sentences. Sometimes
there are two ways of completing the sentence.

1.

> I organize the guitar classes.

I'm responsible *for (organizing) the guitar classes.* .

2.

> Do you ever think it's boring to do that?

Do you ever get bored _____ ?

3.

> No, I always enjoy listening to the guitar, so you shouldn't pity me!

No, I never get tired _____ so you

shouldn't feel sorry _____ .

4.

> I like singing, but I don't think my voice is very good.

I'm very fond _____ , but I'm not very proud _____ .

5.

> The singing teacher here gives marvelous classes. She's quite famous!

The singing teacher here is quite famous _____ .

6.

> Yes, I'm very pleased with all these free lessons.

Yes, I'm grateful _____ .

7.

> You'd better go to bed early. That will help your voice!

If you go to bed early, that will be good _____ .

8.

> But it wouldn't help my social life!

But it would be bad _____ .

3

good bad famous capable responsible	*as* + ROLE	**Examples** She's *famous as* a singer (= SHE IS A SINGER, AND SHE IS FAMOUS) Swimming is *good as* a form of exercise (= SWIMMING IS A FORM OF EXERCISE, AND IT IS A GOOD ONE)

What did they say?
Write *as, of,* or *for* in the blanks.

TED: "I'm best [1] *at* sports photography. Perhaps one day I'll be famous [2]_____ a

sports photographer."

TINA: "People say that swimming is very good [3]_____ you. I'm not bad [4]_____ a

swimmer."

VICKY: "I'm responsible, [5]_____ your guitar teacher, [6]_____ giving you finger exercises.

Lack of exercise is bad [7]_____ a guitarist's fingers."

PAUL: "I don't think I'll ever be famous [8]_____ my singing. I'm just capable [9]_____

singing a tune. But I'm quite good [10]_____ the class comedian!"

18 Mixed practice

1 Here are some facts about Phil Billy, a singer.
Write *about, as, at, for,* or *to* in column 2.

1. He's very good	_at_	singing.
2. But he's also good	_____	an actor.
3. He's very good	_____	his family.
4. He says coffee is bad	_____	his voice.
5. He's always good	_____	any problems during recording.
6. He's just very bad	_____	arriving on time.

2 A hotel receptionist is talking about her work.
In the blanks, write adjectives from the list on the right.
Use each adjective *once.*

You have to be quite ¹_____*good*_____ at speaking English,
French, Spanish, and German. You are ²_____ for the
keys to the rooms, and you have to be ³_____ about
writing down telephone messages exactly. Also, you must be
really ⁴_____ at keeping the list of guests up-to-date.
Some guests are not very easy or pleasant, but you have to be
⁵_____ with the difficult ones. You must at least seem
to be ⁶_____ in their problems, and of course you
must be ⁷_____ to all of them! Naturally, there are
times when I get ⁸_____ of answering all their
questions, and at the end of a difficult day I sometimes feel
quite ⁹_____ of screaming, but I never really get
¹⁰_____ with the work.

bored
capable
careful
efficient
good
interested
patient
polite
responsible
tired

3 Apologies. Two friends are talking.
Choose the right endings from the list below the dialogue.

Hello! I'm so sorry ^{1}___d___ . It's been good ^{2}_____ .

I was worried ^{3}_____ . I'll be interested ^{4}_____ .

I crashed my bike into a pedestrian. At first, I thought he was hurt, but I was wrong ^{5}_____ .

So? What happened? Tell me!

Just be patient ^{6}_____ . A police officer came along and he said I was responsible ^{7}_____ , because I'd been careless ^{8}_____ .

Poor you! I'm beginning to feel sorry ^{9}_____ .

Well, I told the police officer that I was very sorry ^{10}_____ .

And you really were sorry, I'm sure ^{11}_____ .

Yes, so for the next half hour, please be nice ^{12}_____ .

a. about the accident
b. about that
c. about you
d. about being late
e. about signaling
f. for you
g. for the accident
h. of that
i. to me
j. with me
k. in your explanation
l. of you to wait

19 Verbs + prepositions 1

1

listen speak/talk write belong happen	*to*	
ask wait pay look	*for*	(= TRY TO FIND)

look	*at*	
look	*after*	(= TAKE CARE OF)

Examples
Something nice happened *to* me today.
I'm looking *for* my hat.
I'm looking *at* some interesting photographs.
I'm looking *after* their baby today.

Ted is telling Sue about a terrible restaurant he went to.
Write a preposition in each blank.

Just listen ¹___to___ this. To begin with, I had to wait twenty

minutes ²_____ the waitress. When I asked her

³_____ the menu, she had to go and look ⁴_____ it;

there was only one, and something had happened ⁵_____

it. Then, when I spoke ⁶_____ her she didn't listen

⁷_____ me, so she brought some cheese which I didn't want.

I hadn't asked ⁸_____ it, but she wanted me to pay

⁹_____ it! The restaurant belongs ¹⁰_____ Tamara

Lane, the TV cooking expert. I'll write ¹¹_____ her. The

waitresses really should look ¹²_____ the customers

better.

2

speak/talk write complain	(to someone)	*about*	+ noun + *doing something*
tell	someone		
think/dream		*about/of*	

Examples
She talked *about* Spain/*about traveling* in Spain.
He's thinking *about/of* a vacation to Europe/*about going* to Europe.

Note
Tell must take an indirect object:
Tell *us* about your vacation.
(NOT: Tell about your vacation.)

In the terrible restaurant.
Complete the descriptions. Use the verbs in italics.

1. Where's the waitress? I don't *have* any bread.

   A is going to complain ___*to the waitress about not having any bread.*___

2. One day I'll *have* my own restaurant.

   B is dreaming _____

3. I've *found* a piece of string in my soup! The waitress should know about this!

   C is going to tell _____

4. The chef here doesn't know how to *cook* vegetables. I want to tell him . . .

   D wants to talk _____

5. I think the Health Department should *close* this restaurant.

   I'll send them a letter.

   E is going to write _____

6. Perhaps I should *look* for another job.

   The waitress is thinking _____

3 Write some sentences about your last summer vacation, or ask the
questions and write about your partner's vacation.

1. Did you speak to anyone interesting? About what?

   _____

2. Did you buy anything special? How much did you pay for it?

   I paid _____

3. Did you or anyone else complain about anything? To whom?

   _____

4. Did you write to anyone? About what?

   _____

5. What will you do during your next summer vacation?

   I'm thinking _____

20 Verbs + prepositions 2

1

run/bump	*into*	I *ran into* a friend yesterday (= WE MET BY CHANCE)
run/bump/crash	*into*	The car *ran into* the wall (= IT HAD AN ACCIDENT)
run	*over*	The car *ran over* a cat (= IT KNOCKED THE CAT DOWN AND DROVE OVER IT)
run/drive, etc.	*after*	The police officer *ran after* the thief (= HE FOLLOWED THE THIEF WHILE RUNNING)
catch up	*with*	The police officer ran fast and *caught up with* the thief (= THE POLICE OFFICER WAS BEHIND AT FIRST, BUT THEN HE REACHED THE SAME PLACE AS THE THIEF)

■ Tina and Paul took part in a cross-country bicycle race.
Complete the description of what happened.

1. Another cyclist ___ran into___ Tina.

2. So Tina nearly _____ a small boy.

3. The father _____ her.

4. But he couldn't _____ her.

5. Paul nearly _____ a tree.

6. After the race, Tina _____ a friend from college.

2 shout throw	*at*	(= ANGRILY) (= WANTING TO HIT SOMEONE OR SOMETHING) They shouted *at* the thief and threw stones *at* him.
shout throw	*to*	(= WANTING THE OTHER PERSON TO HEAR) (= SO THAT THE OTHER PERSON CAN CATCH) She shouted *to* me that I should come upstairs, and threw the key down *to* me.
laugh smile stare	*at*	First the children stared *at* the comedian; then they laughed *at* his jokes.
point wave	*at/to*	She pointed *at/to* the sign on the door. The film star waved *at/to* the crowd.

Find a suitable ending in column 3 for each sentence.

1. I might	stare	a. to a small child.
2.	wave	b. at a strange person.
3.	throw a ball	c. at a good joke.
4.	shout	d. at a friend in another car.
5.	laugh	e. at something I wanted to buy.
6.	point	f. to a friend in another room.

Answers: 1. _____ , 2. _____ , 3. _____ , 4. _____ , 5. _____ , 6. _____

3 Things that happened at the bicycle race.
Write prepositions from Exercises 1 and 2 in the spaces.

1. Tina shouted ¹__to__ the small boy that he should stay off the road.

2. The boy's father was very angry, so he shouted ²_____ Tina and threw a stone ³_____ her.

3. The other people stared ⁴_____ him and pointed ⁵_____ Tina.

4. The father wanted a police car to drive ⁶_____ Tina, but the police officer only smiled ⁷_____ him.

5. When Tina saw her friend, she waved ⁸_____ her and shouted "Hello!" ⁹_____ her.

㉑ Verbs + prepositions 3

1

		+ noun	+ *doing*	
apply	*for*	√	—	
apologize		√	√	
reply	*to*	√	—	
look forward		√	√	
hear	*from*	√	—	(= RECEIVE NEWS FROM SOMEONE IN A LETTER, BY TELEPHONE, ETC.)
consist	*of*	√	√	
call	*on*	√	—	(= VISIT SOMEONE FORMALLY)
drop in		√	—	(= VISIT SOMEONE INFORMALLY OR UNEXPECTEDLY)

Examples
He apologized *for* his mistake/*for making* that mistake.
I'm looking forward *to* my new job/*to starting* my new job.
A knife consists *of* a handle and a blade.
His job as a tour guide consists *of taking* tourists around the town and *answering* their questions.

Note
The verbs *ask, answer, call,* and *phone* are often used without a preposition.
    They couldn't *answer the teacher.*
    I'll *call/phone your secretary.*

Find a suitable ending in column 2 for each sentence.

Usually:
1. We reply
2. We look forward
3. We are pleased when we hear
4. We also enjoy calling
5. We drop in
6. We apologize
7. We apply
8. Our lives consist

a. from our friends.
b. for being late.
c. on old friends and relatives.
d. to people's letters.
e. of work, home life, and leisure.
f. to going on vacation.
g. our friends.
h. for jobs.

1. __d__ , 2. ____ , 3. ____ , 4. ____ , 5. ____ , 6. ____ , 7. ____ , 8. ____

2

to be	employed qualified involved	*in*	+ noun (e.g., medicine)	*as*	(ROLE OR POSITION) *(e.g., a doctor)*
			+ *doing* (e.g., teaching)		

Examples
He's employed *in* the oil industry *as* an engineer.
She's involved *in* traveling to many countries *as* a business executive.

Tina decided to apply for a job at the music school during her spring break. In each blank, write a preposition from Exercise 1 or 2, or write a dash (—).

Dear Sirs,

I would like to apply ¹___for___ the job of music assistant, which you advertised recently. I apologize ²_____ applying rather late. When I called ³_____ your secretary, she said I could still apply.

I am not employed ⁴_____ teaching, but I am qualified ⁵_____ an advanced guitar player and I am involved ⁶_____ teaching the guitar ⁷_____ a helper in a youth club. My work in the youth club consists ⁸_____ helping the staff generally and some teaching.

I hope you will be interested in my application, and am looking forward ⁹_____ hearing ¹⁰_____ you.

Sincerely,

Tina Brown

3 Write your own application for a job you would like.

_____

_____

_____

_____

_____

22 Verbs + prepositions 4

1

| concentrate
decide
depend
rely
insist
work | *on* | + noun
+ *doing* | **Examples**
She was concentrating *on* her
book/*on reading* her book.
They were working *on* the car.
(e.g., making or repairing it)
They were working *on getting* the
car ready by 5:00. (= WERE
MAKING AN EFFORT TO ACHIEVE
THIS) |

Paul has made this list of things that he will do and will not do
when he returns home.
Write what he is thinking.

1. I'll insist *on getting my dictionary back from Bill.*

2. I'll decide _____

3. I'll work _____

4. I'll concentrate _____

5. I won't rely _____

1. Dictionary. Get back from Bill.
2. Possible career. Decide.
3. Must improve my essay techniques.
4. Must pass exams.
5. Not study at the last minute.

2 All these verbs need a direct object before the preposition.

	Direct object			**Examples**
invite	someone	*to*	+ noun	They invited *me to* their party.
provide	someone	*with*		She borrowed *a book from* a friend.
borrow	something	*from*		
accuse	someone	*of*	+ noun	They accused *him of* the crime/*of stealing* the money.
blame	someone/something	*for*	+ *(not) doing*	I congratulate *you on* your success/*on winning* the race.
congratulate	someone	*on*		
protect	someone	*from*		They warned *us about* the danger/*about* swimming near the rocks.
spend	something	*on*		
warn	someone	*about*		

Tina is writing to her cousin about a lesson in windsurfing.
Write a preposition in each blank.

You certainly can't accuse me [1] __of__ being lazy! One of

the instructors here invited me [2] _____ a windsurfing

lesson, after a whole day's tennis, and I said "Yes!" Of course, at

home I would have to spend a lot of money [3] _____ buying

equipment, but I borrowed a wet suit [4] _____ the instructor.

Naturally, they provided students [5] _____ the sailboard. I

didn't need a crash helmet to protect me [6] _____ the

sailboard. Really, the sailboard needed to be protected

[7] _____ me! The instructor reminded me to position

my feet correctly, and warned me [8] _____ not

letting go of the boom, but . . . ! Anyway, he didn't blame me

[9] _____ falling in, and he even congratulated me

[10] _____ not falling through the sail!

3 Finish these sentences. Write a direct object if necessary, the
preposition, and the verb in parentheses in its correct form.

1. When Tina fell in, the instructor didn't blame ___her for___

   ___falling_____ in. (fall)

2. Tina insisted _____

   again. (try)

3. He also warned _____ onto

   the sailboard. (not jump)

4. This time she concentrated _____

   _____ the boom firmly. (hold)

5. He congratulated _____

   so quickly. (learn)

23 Mixed practice

1 Charles works in the personnel department of a large company. How does he spend the day? In each blank, write a preposition, or a dash (—) if there should be no preposition.

For much of the day, Charles listens ^{1}___to___ people. They tell ^{2}_____ him ^{3}_____ their problems or their ambitions. He answers ^{4}_____ their questions. Sometimes they complain ^{5}_____ him ^{6}_____ their bosses. That's difficult for Charles. He can't reply easily ^{7}_____ a person who asks ^{8}_____ him ^{9}_____ help about a bad boss. Charles says, "My work consists ^{10}_____ listening a lot, saying a little, and smiling ^{11}_____ nearly everyone who comes in!"

2 Charles is on the telephone.
Find the right ending for each sentence. Write your answers below.

1. So two weeks ago you applied	a. to your letter.
2. But you still haven't heard	b. for that.
3. It seems that we didn't reply	c. for a job with us.
4. Well, I do apologize	d. from us.
5. Actually, I'm sure that we answered	e. of lying!
6. I remember, we wrote	f. your letter.
7. No! I'm not accusing you	g. to you three days ago.

1. __C__ , 2. _____ , 3. _____ , 4. _____ , 5. _____ , 6. _____ , 7. _____

3 Charles is still on the telephone.
Find the right ending for each sentence. Write your answers below.

1. Yes! I'm listening	a. in starting our new computer.
2. You see, we've been very involved	b. to seeing you.
3. We've been concentrating	c. with a new application form.
4. Oh, you're qualified	d. on us tomorrow to get it?
5. Anyway, we must provide you	e. as a computer programmer.
6. Could you drop in	f. on learning to use it.
7. And this time you can depend	g. us.
8. So I look forward	h. to you.
9. And thank you for calling	i. on us to reply.

1. __h__ , 2. _____ , 3. _____ , 4. _____ , 5. _____ , 6. _____ , 7. _____ , 8. _____ ,

9. _____

50

4 After a concert. People are waiting to see the singer Contessa when she comes out of the theater.
Write a preposition or a dash (—) in each space.

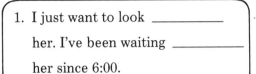

1. I just want to look _____ her. I've been waiting _____ her since 6:00.

6. Why isn't she here? What's happened _____ her?

7. I'm going to ask _____ her _____ a photograph. Anyway, I'll try to speak _____ her.

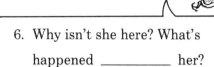

2. A lot of rude people will stare _____ her and shout _____ her. But *I'm* just going to smile _____ her and wave _____ her.

8. Those two enormous men protect her _____ the crowds; they look _____ her.

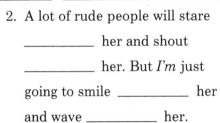

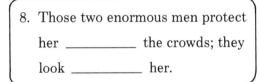

3. I spent a lot of money _____ my ticket, and I'm going to insist _____ seeing her.

9. What? She's gone! She left by another door! I'm going to complain _____ the theater _____ that!

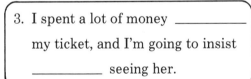

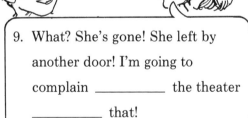

4. I want to congratulate her _____ a marvelous show. But will she listen _____ me?

10. Oh well. She was probably tired. You can't blame her _____ being tired.

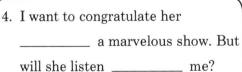

5. That enormous car belongs _____ her. How much did she pay _____ it, I wonder?

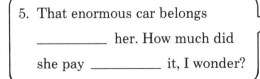

24 Usual phrases 1

1

a	visit	*to*	**Examples** his visit *to* Africa/*to* the doctor.
	plan	*for*	our plans *for* our vacation/*for* you.
	meeting	*with* *between* *of*	The students had a meeting *with* the professor. There was a meeting *between* the students and the professor. There was a meeting *of* the new students.
a	book letter talk/lecture program (on TV or radio)	*on*[1] *about*[2]	a book *on/about* Brazil; *on/about traveling* in Brazil some advice *on/about* the problem; *on/about solving* the problem
some	advice ideas		

Notes
[1]We usually use *on* for formal or specialized books, or when we are using a more formal
   style of English:
   The professor wrote a letter to the newspaper *on* the country's economic situation.
[2]We usually use *about* for more informal or general books, or when we are using a more informal
   style of English:
   My cousin wrote me a letter *about* his trip.

Ted has made a list of things he must do when he returns to
New York. He's telling Sue about them.
Fill in the blanks.

"When I get back, I have to attend a meeting ¹___of___ the

Photography Club; prepare plans ²_____ the Club's visit

³_____ Boston; send the Tourist Bureau a

letter ⁴_____ our visit; get some advice ⁵_____

transportation; and find a good book ⁶_____ architectural

photography. Do you have any ideas ⁷_____ unusual buildings

we can photograph? No? Oh well, there's a TV program

⁸_____ Boston the night before we go. Oh, and I want

to arrange a meeting ⁹_____ the University's Camera Club.

Well, all that will keep me busy!"

> Photography Club
> Meeting
> Re: Club visit to
>   Boston. Todo:
> 1. Prepare plans
> 2. Write Boston
>   Tourist Bureau
> 3. Transportation-get advice
> 4. Architectural photography
>   -find good book
> 5. Unusual buildings in
>   Boston. Sue: any ideas?
> 6. July 30: Watch TV-
>   "Boston Architecture."
> 7. University Camera Club:
>   try to meet members?

2

a	question reply/answer	*to* *about*	**Examples** That was his question *to* her *about* the trip/*about planning* the trip.
	reason need	*for*	Is there any need *for* silence/*for being* silent?
	cause result cost/price way	*of*	His success was the result *of* hard work/*of working* hard. This is my way *of* frying eggs.
	rise/increase fall/decrease	*in*	Last year there was an increase *in* the number of tourists here.

Some time later, Ted received this letter from a bus company.
Fill in the blanks.

Dear Sir,

This letter is in reply [1] __to__ your letter of August 15. The reason [2] _____ the rise [3] _____ the cost [4] _____ hiring a bus is the recent increase [5] _____ the price [6] _____ gas. This increase, as you know, has been the result [7] _____ problems in the oil industry. We do understand the need [8] _____ inexpensive transportation for your club, and we feel sure that you will not find a cheaper way [9] _____ taking your members to Boston. Of course, if there is a fall [10] _____ the price of gas, there will be a decrease [11] _____ our charge to you.

Sincerely yours,

D A Cotten

Comfort Bus Company

3

Complete this list about yourself or a partner. Use prepositions from the tables. For example:
I would be interested in a meeting *with* the President.

I would be interested in these things:

a meeting _____   a TV program _____

a visit _____   a talk _____

a book _____

25 Usual phrases 2

1

to be	*at*	work school college home
		in/at church *in* bed *in* college *in/at* the hospital

to	go come	*to*	work school college church bed
		to/into the hospital	
		home	

Examples
He's *at* work today, although it's a holiday.
My sister is going *to* college next year.
The children are *in* bed. They went *to* bed early.
My father's *at* home. He *came home* a few minutes ago.

Notes
We used *to be in college/school* to mean *to be attending college/ school.*
When he was *in college,* he had many friends.
With all the words above (except *work*) we use *the* or *a* if we are referring to a particular school, church, bed, etc.
With the word *hospital, the* or *a* is always used.
He was *in the bed* by the window.
A professor *in the college* spoke to us.
My father went *to the home* of some friends this evening.

■ What they said at a party.
Put one or two words, or a dash (—) in each blank.

TINA: "Yes, my brother's still [1]___*in*___ high school, but he wants to go [2]_____ college when he's eighteen. I'm [3]_____ college myself. I go [4]_____ college on the east coast."

TED: "After my football accident I had to go [5]_____ hospital for a while. I was [6]_____ hospital for three days, and then I spent another week [7]_____ bed [8]_____ home."

PAUL: "I'm hoping to have a job next summer. There are jobs [9]_____ hospital near my home. I go [10]_____ school which helps you to find summer jobs."

SUE: "In thirty-six hours I'll be back [11]_____ work in New York. I'm really looking forward to going [12]_____ home. I'm going [13]_____ church tomorrow. I'd like to go [14]_____ church where the singing is really good."

2

to have (something)	*for*	breakfast lunch, etc.
to be/go, etc.	*on*	vacation business
to be/speak, etc.	*on*	the telphone/phone the radio TV
to go/come	*for*	a run a swim, etc.

The manager of a young tennis star is having a telephone conversation with a reporter.
Write a preposition in each blank.

1. Yes, Rob is here ___*on*___ vacation, not _____ business.

2. No, he can't speak to you _____ the phone.

3. Yes, he did go _____ a run this morning.

4. He had two oranges and a boiled egg _____ breakfast.

5. No, I don't know what he had _____ dinner yesterday.

6. Yes, he might go _____ a swim later today.

7. You'll see him _____ TV tomorrow, and he'll have an interview _____ the radio on Monday.

3 Complete each of these questions with one or two words.
Then answer them yourself, or ask a partner to answer them.

1. Where would you most like to go _____ vacation?

2. What do you most enjoy doing _____ home?

3. What do/did you most enjoy _____ school?

4. What would you most like to have _____ lunch or dinner on your birthday?

5. How much time do you usually spend _____ telephone in a week?

6. Have you ever been _____ a swim in the moonlight?

26 Usual phrases 3

1	a	book, play, etc. painting, drawing, etc. song, symphony, etc.	*by*	Shakespeare Picasso Mozart

These sentences are nonsense! Rearrange the words in columns
3 and 5, and write down true sentences.

	is a(n)		by	
1. Hamlet		painting		Lennon and McCartney.
2. Yesterday		novel		Mozart.
3. War and Peace		play		Leonardo da Vinci.
4. The Mona Lisa		opera		Michelangelo.
5. David		statue		Tolstoy.
6. Don Giovanni		song		Shakespeare.

1. _Hamlet is a play by Shakespeare._

2. _____

3. _____

4. _____

5. _____

6. _____

2	*in*	danger love (with)	*out of*	danger work order	(= WITHOUT A JOB) He lost his job and is now *out of work.* (= NOT FUNCTIONING) I dropped the telephone and now it's *out of order.*
	indoors				
			outdoors		

Complete the sentences below to fill in the words in this puzzle.

1. Office workers spend most of their time _____ . (one word)

2. An unemployed person is _____ . (three words)

3. If a person has a temperature of 107°F, his/her life is _____ . (two
   words)

4. Most people are _____ when they marry. (two words)

5. A farmer spends a lot of his time _____ . (one word)

6. If your telephone is broken, it is out of _____ . (one word)

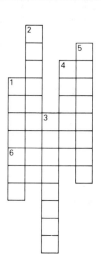

3

| on | purpose
my/your, etc. own |
| by | mistake
myself/yourself, etc. |
| in | charge
a hurry |

| up-to | -date | (= MODERN)
an up-to-date dictionary |
| out-of | | (= NOT MODERN, NO LONGER SUITABLE OR CORRECT) |

Fill in the blanks to complete this information.

Paul wants to move to a college with a modern computer
department, where there is ¹ _up-to_ -date equipment. He
says, "I tried to call the college for information, but I got the wrong
number, because the telephone directory was ² _____ -date.
The person who answered was rather angry, so I said, 'Look, I got
your number ³ _____ mistake. I certainly haven't bothered
you ⁴ _____ purpose.' "

Tina is ⁵ _____ a hurry to leave her school. She would like a
job where she is ⁶ _____ charge of the arrangements for
musicians from abroad. She would like to live ⁷ _____ her
own for some time, but she says, "I probably couldn't pay the
rent ⁸ _____ myself."

4 Answer these questions about yourself, or ask a partner to answer
them.
Five years from now, what do you think?
1. Will you spend most of your time indoors or outdoors?
2. Will you be in charge of any other people?
3. Will you be in love?
4. Will you be living on your own?
Begin your sentences like this:
I think I will . . .
. . . thinks he/she will . . .

1. _____
2. _____
3. _____
4. _____

27 Mixed practice

1 Lee is in her first job. She is in the office, writing a letter to a friend.
Complete the sentences from her letter, using each item below only *once*.
Use a dash (—) if there should be no word.

> (—) for for in in in into on out of

1. Three of the people here were _____*in*_____ college just before
   they joined the company.

2. Two of the people here go _____ a swim before work every day.

3. I always stay _____ bed until the last minute, so I have
   only a cup of coffee _____ breakfast.

4. At the end of the day, most of the staff go straight _____
   home, but I'd like to do something more exciting!

5. We can't use the computer today because its _____ order.

6. My neighbor's having a long conversation _____ the phone.

7. One of the men had to go _____ the hospital for an operation.

8. Some of the staff are going to visit him while he's _____ the hospital.

2 Write the opposite of the expressions in italics. Fill in each blank
with *one* word.

1. Lee isn't *at home* today. She's _____*at*_____ _____*work*_____ .

2. There hasn't been a *rise in* the number of unemployed people.
   There has been a _____ _____ the number.

3. You didn't do that *by mistake!* You did it _____
   _____ .

4. He didn't want to be *indoors* on that lovely day. He wanted to
   be _____.

5. She didn't go to Hawaii *on vacation.* She went _____
   _____ .

6. Last month there was an *increase in* the price of fruit, but this
   month there has been a _____ _____ the price.

7. This list of prices is *out-of-date.* I need a list that is _____
   _____ _____ .

3 These are three sets of headings from a magazine. Complete the explanations. Write a preposition in each blank.

1. The doctor in charge ____of____ medical research, in a

   reply _____ questions, said, "We do not know the cause

   _____ this new illness. We must find a way _____

   curing it, and there is a need _____ research. But we

   must not act _____ a hurry. This is an international

   problem, and we cannot act _____ ourselves."

2. This article _____ Helen Venables is _____ her

   voyage around the world _____ her own. The low cost

   _____ the voyage was the result _____ gifts from

   several large organizations.

3. A reporter has had a meeting _____ Rocket Ronson, who

   is on a visit _____ the United States. Ronson talked

   about his plans _____ a new tournament and explained

   his reasons _____ wanting a new tournament.

---

(1) Mysterious new illness

Doctor responsible for medical research answers questions. "We do not know causes. Research is needed. Cannot act quickly. Must act with other nations."

---

(2) Helen Venables writes.

"How I sailed around the world alone, for $1,000." Big organizations were generous.

---

(3) Rocket Ronson, world's No. 1 tennis champion, in the U.S.

Planning a new international tournament. Why?

---

4 How would you feel about doing these things? Complete each question. Then answer the questions yourself, or ask another student to answer them. For example: How would you feel about staying at home for three days without going out?
Check (√) one box in reply to each question.

	OK	Not OK	It depends
1. Spend three days __at__ home without going out.			
2. Spend three nights _____ in a tent.			
3. Cook a dinner for four people _____ yourself.			
4. Get dressed for an important party _____ a hurry.			
5. Pay a visit _____ a house full of people whom you don't know.			
6. Write a magazine article _____ someone you know.			

Answer Key

1 Where? 1 (pages 6 and 7)

1
2. on   3. at   4. next to   5. opposite
6. far from   7. far from   8. at   9. next
10. opposite

2
2. on top of   3. on   4. at the top of
5. above   6. below

2 Where? 2 (pages 8 and 9)

1
2. in the back of   3. on the left
4. on the right of   5. in the front

2
2. outside   3. around   4. in front of
5. beside   6. behind

3
2. on   3. above   4. Through   5. on   6. on
7. in a corner of   8. in

3 Where? 3 (pages 10 and 11)

1
1. False. Woods Hole is north of Edgartown.
2. True   3. True   4. False. Woods Hole is on
the coast of Massachusetts.   5. False.
Vineyard Haven is north of Tisbury.

2
2. west   3. in   4. on   5. in   6. north
7. from   8. in the south/in the southeast

3
2. in   3. in   4. on   5. on   6. in   7. on

4
2. on/by   3. on   4. on top of   5. off   6. in
7. off

4 Mixed practice (pages 12 and 13)

1

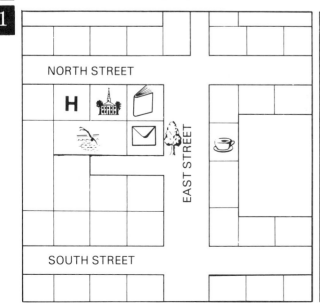

2

1. at the top   2. at the bottom   3. on the left
4. on the right   5. on/on top of   6. beside/
next to   7. above   8. below   9. in/inside
10. outside

3
2. above/over   3. on   4. behind   5. on
6. in   7. at   8. on   9. off/near   10. from
11. near   12. from   13. far from   14. on
15. north/northwest   16. in the south of

5 Direction 1 (pages 14 and 15)

1
2. from   3. along   4. toward   5. right
6. past   7. as far as   8. left onto   9. left

2
2. elevator   3. stairs   4. stairs
5. hallway/corridor   6. door   7. closet

3
2. up   3. along   4. into   5. out of   6. down
7. through   8. into

6 Direction 2 (pages 16 and 17)

1
2. through   3. along   4. over   5. around
6. across   7. under

2
2. around   3. over   4. along   5. through
6. across   7. under

3
2. into   3. across   4. out of   5. over/across
6. across   7. over   8. onto   9. off   10. onto

7 Direction 3 (pages 18 and 19)

1
2. in   3. to   4. to   5. to   6. at/in   7. to

2 2. to   3. to   4. in/at   5. to   6. in   7. for   8. at

3 2. as far as   3. through/into   4. into   5. out of   6. toward   7. from   8. to

8 Mixed practice (pages 20 and 21)

1 2. through   3. past   4. around   5. over/across   6. across/over   7. around   8. along   9. through   10. onto   11. through   12. along   13. toward   14. onto   15. over   16. across/over   17. past   18. as far as

2 2. over   3. onto   4. into   5. through   6. in   7. out of   8. off   9. on   10. down   11. from   12. across   13. up   14. into

3 2. in   3. to   4. for   5. to   6. in   7. to

9 When? 1 (pages 22 and 23)

1 2. in   3. in   4. on   5. in   6. In   7. On   8. on   9. in   10. On   11. on/at   12. on   13. in

2 3. —   4. On   5. —   6. in   7. —

3 2. at   3. at   4. in   5. In   6. at   7. —   8. —   9. at

10 When? 2 (pages 24 and 25)

1 2. for   3. since   4. after   5. from, to/until   6. during   7. for   8. for   9. for   10. since

2 2. by   3. to/until   4. until   5. by   6. until   7. by   8. to/until

11 Mixed practice (pages 26 and 27)

1 2. before   3. by   4. from   5. to/until   6. until   7. at   8. in   9. from   10. to/until   11. after

2 2. since   3. from   4. to/until   5. during   6. for   7. for   8. —   9. on   10. —   11. for/—   12. —   13. until

3 A suggested text: Contessa was born in Pasadena on May 10, 1965. She went to school in 1970 and stayed there until 1982, and hated it. In 1975 she began singing in a church choir, and stayed in the choir for five years. By 1980 she had already made three records—for the church! In 1982 she began singing with a local group called the Pebbles, and stayed with them until 1984. On August 4, 1983 she sang in a show in Las Vegas. A Mammoth Records producer was in the audience. Two weeks later, she signed a contract with Mammoth Records. She has been under contract with Mammoth since then. In 1988 and 1989 she had two gold records. Contessa says, "I have been singing for other people for 15 years, but I really sing for myself." She plans to make a third gold record (by her 25th birthday)! I checked the charts last Saturday, and it seems possible.

12 How? (pages 28 and 29)

1 2. by   3. on the   4. by   5. by   6. by   7. on the   8. by   9. in the   10. on   11. in his   12. by   13. on the/that   14. by/on a   15. on an/his

2 2. of   3. by   4. with   5. by   6. out of   7. of   8. with   9. out of   10. of   11. by   12. with

13 What are they like? (pages 30 and 31)

1 2. curly hair   3. a white blouse   4. a guitar   5. at least 25   6. a small moustache   7. a small black hat   8. a cane   9. about 16   10. dark glasses   11. an amazing hairstyle   12. a strange bag

2 2. like   3. as   4. like   5. like   6. like   7. as   8. like   9. as   10. like   11. like

14 Mixed practice (pages 32 and 33)

1 2. of   3. as   4. by   5. out of   6. as   7. like   8. by   9. out of   10. as

3 2. with   3. in   4. out of   5. like   6. with
7. on   8. like   9. of   10. with   11. in
12. of   13. with   14. on   15. like   16. of
17. with   18. in   19. like   20. as   21. in

15 Adjectives + prepositions 1 (pages 34 and 35)

1 2. to   3. about   4. about   5. to   6. to
7. about   8. of   9. about   10. to
11. to   12. to   13. about   14. to   15. about
16. of

2 2. about/that   3. with them   4. with us
5. about that   6. with us   7. about him/that
8. about it/that   9. about it/that
10. about it/that

3 3. about waiting for them   4. about winning it
5. about playing in it
6. about not writing to you

16 Adjectives + prepositions 2 (pages 36 and 37)

1 2. at   3. at   4. of   5. of   6. of   7. at
8. of   9. in

2 2. at putting up a tent?
3. of trying dangerous sports?
4. in meeting lots of different people?
5. at learning new skills?

17 Adjectives + prepositions 3 (pages 38 and 39)

1 B. 1   C. 6   D. 2   E. 3   F. 5   G. 4

2 2. with (doing) that?   3. of (listening to) the
guitar; for me   4. of singing; of my voice
5. for her marvelous classes/for giving
marvelous classes   6. for all these free
lessons   7. for your voice   8. for my social
life!

3 2. as   3. for   4. as   5. as   6. for   7. for
8. for   9. of   10. as

18 Mixed practice (pages 40 and 41)

1 2. as   3. to   4. for   5. about   6. at

2 2. responsible   3. careful   4. efficient
5. patient   6. interested   7. polite   8. tired
9. capable   10. bored

3 2. l   3. c   4. k   5. b   6. j   7. g   8. e   9. f
10. a   11. b/h   12. i

19 Verbs + prepositions 1 (pages 42 and 43)

1 2. for   3. for   4. for   5. to   6. to   7. to
8. for   9. for   10. to   11. to   12. after

2 2. about/of having her own restaurant   3. the
waitress about finding a piece of string in his
soup   4. to the chef about cooking
vegetables   5. to the Health Department
about closing this/the restaurant   6. about
looking for another job

20 Verbs + prepositions 2 (pages 44 and 45)

1 2. ran over   3. ran after   4. catch up with
5. ran/crashed/bumped into
6. ran/bumped into

2 2. d   3. a   4. f   5. c   6. e

3 2. at   3. at   4. at   5. at/to   6. after   7. at
8. at/to   9. to

21 Verbs + prepositions 3 (pages 46 and 47)

1 2. f   3. a   4. c/g   5. c   6. b   7. h   8. e

2 2. for   3. —   4. in   5. as   6. in   7. as
8. of   9. to   10. from

22 Verbs + prepositions 4 (pages 48 and 49)

1 2. on a possible career   3. on (improving) my
essay techniques   4. on (passing) the exams
5. on studying at the last minute

2 2. to/(for)   3. on   4. from   5. with   6. from
7. from   8. about   9. for   10. on

3 2. on trying   3. her about not jumping
4. on holding   5. her on learning

Answer Key

23 Mixed practice (pages 50 and 51)

1 2. — 3. about 4. — 5. to 6. about
7. to 8. — 9. for 10. of 11. at

2 2. d 3. a 4. b 5. f 6. g 7. e

3 2. a 3. f 4. e 5. c 6. d 7. i 8. b 9. g

4 1. for 2. at, at, at, at/to 3. on, on 4. on, to
5. to, for 6. to 7. —, for, to
8. from, after 9. to, about 10. for

24 Usual phrases 1 (pages 52 and 53)

1 2. for 3. to 4. about 5. on/about
6. on/about 7. on/about 8. on/about
9. with

2 2. for 3. in 4. of 5. in 6. of 7. of
8. for 9. of 10. in 11. in

25 Usual phrases 2 (pages 54 and 55)

1 2. to 3. at/in 4. to a 5. to the 6. in the
7. in 8. at 9. at a/in a 10. to a 11. at
12. — 13. to 14. to a

2 1. on 2. on 3. for 4. for 5. for 6. for
7. on, on

3 1. on 2. at 3. at/in 4. for 5. on the
6. for

26 Usual phrases 3 (pages 56 and 57)

1 2. Yesterday—song—Lennon and McCartney
3. War and Peace—novel—Tolstoy
4. The Mona Lisa—painting—Leonardo da Vinci
5. David—statue—Michelangelo
6. Don Giovanni—opera—Mozart

2 1. indoors 2. out of work 3. in danger
4. in love 5. outdoors 6. order

3 2. out-of 3. by 4. on 5. in 6. in 7. on
8. by

27 Mixed practice (pages 58 and 59)

1 2. for 3. in, for 4. — 5. out of 6. on
7. to/into 8. in

2 2. fall in/decrease in 3. on purpose
4. outdoors 5. on business 6. decrease in/
fall in 7. up-to-date

3 1. to, of, of, for, in, by 2. by, about/on, on,
of, of 3. with, to, for, for

4 2. outdoors 3. by 4. in 5. to 6. about/on